George Scarbro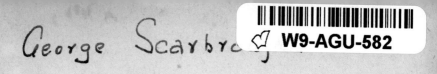

GAUTAMA THE ENLIGHTENED

and other verse

GAUTAMA
THE ENLIGHTENED
and other verse

BY

JOHN MASEFIELD

NEW YORK

THE MACMILLAN COMPANY

1941

FIRST PRINTING.

Scarbrough

g

12-5-55 rc
1-27-56 cdm

PRINTED IN THE UNITED STATES OF AMERICA
AMERICAN BOOK—STRATFORD PRESS, INC., NEW YORK

CONTENTS

GAUTAMA THE ENLIGHTENED

Invocation

O MASTER of the Calmness, come
Forth from the shadow of the tree,
Gladden the joyless who are dumb
And make the blind to see,
That, in the tiger in his rage,
And in the summer fly
Alike, in struggle on his stage
A brother passes by,
Till, from the fires of the art
There flash the perfect ring,
Or through the violet's golden heart
He pass into the Spring.

"I am the Prince Siddartha, the King's son.
My Father rules the Sakya warriors
Here in this palace of Kapilavastu
Wherein, for seven hundred years, his forebears
Have been the Kings; where I shall be the King.

Of all lives known to me, my life has been
The happiest, hitherto; I have known no-one
Not valiant, not made beautiful by thought,
Not gentle from an inner ecstasy.
All who have taught and trained me have been wise,
Brave, swift in justice, merciful in blame,
Striving to fit me to be King of men.

[1]

Because, in time (thus the tale goes), my Father
Will gird his sword about him and take horse
And shake the Sakya bannerol and ride
West, to the palace where his forebears dwell,
And be with them forever, and myself
Will rule the Sakya kingdom in his stead.

And, of all lives of men, what happier is
Or can be, than to seek a Kingdom's love,
To watch over and guard a City's fate,
And guide a Nation's fortunes happily?
To rid it of oppression and misrule,
To give its citizens a share in all things,
So that they all are beautiful in body,
Alert in mind, in knowledge excellent,
And in their spirits companied with angels?
My lot it is to be this blessed thing
A King of men; a wondrous lot is mine.

And now, today, I stand upon a threshold,
For here, today, two princes come to try
If one of them, or I, deserve the prize.
We are to struggle for the mastery
And he who wins will marry the Princess,
The Princess Yasodhara, whom men call
The Rose of all the Beauty of the East.
O may my spirit, mind and hand be sure
That I may make this earthly wonder mine.

If it be granted to my skill to win;
If the Princess be mine, there will be feast,

I shall be married to that lovely spirit
One more surpassing ecstasy made mine.

Surely, the Life of Man is beautiful
Beyond all telling; I have never seen
Anything, yet, that is not beautiful.
Outside this palace of my ancestors
Are fragrant flower-gardens, fruit-tree-groves,
Cool fish-ponds sparkling with the fountain-splash,
Then the great river, then the hills, then mountains
Snowy forever in the northern heaven.
Wherever the eye looks deep beauty dwells.

And loveliness is in the people here.
Beautiful childen play about the palace,
The waiting-maidens sing; they are like flowers,
And like gazelles for grace, like birds for mirth;
The men-at-arms are marvellous in strength,
Swift spearmen, mighty bowmen, runners, wrestlers,
Glowing with health and merry in their courage.
And beautiful are those clear, eager spirits
Who teach me wisdom that is like a spring
In a green forest giving life to all things.

And I, who live amid this happiness,
And may be happier still, and may be King,
And may be happier beyond count in making
My people happy, shall have still a joy
Before me, when the golden morning comes
And I take horse and ride west to the palace
To find my Father and his forebears gathered

And dwell with them forever in great bliss
Leaving my Son to rule the Kingdom here.
That is the end of Life, my teachers tell me.
So that all Life is exquisite, God wot.

In a few moments, I must meet the princes
In contest for the hand of the Princess.
I shall be winner of the contest, surely,
For all my Destiny seems happiness . . .

And yet, there is another happiness.

I recollect a day in early childhood.
After the rain, I went with other boys,
Into the fields, when all were full of flowers.
We went past a still water where the cranes
White, with red plumes, stood silent in the stream
Watching, while dragon-flies gleamed by, and snakes
Panted with flicking tongues on the hot stone.
The water-mice clambered the iris stalks
To their inwove grass-houses; the fish splashed,
The little deer their dainty muzzles dipped.

There was a flower of mingled red and white
So marvellous in form, colour and scent
That, looking at it there, I was aware
Of a white planet in a winter dawn
And of cocks crying at an unseen herald,
And then of Joy so great that all was joy.
In joy I understood and shared all life.
I was the living soul in everything.

[4]

I have not told of this. I have asked friends
To name their dear delights, but never yet
Heard one describe a happiness like that
Which was a passing into the world's heart.

There must be ways of entering that joy.
About us are the doors of Paradise
A million barred, a million never barred.
How find an unbarred door and enter in?

And yet, I have sufficient happiness.
And now the princes wait to struggle with me
I will go pit my power against theirs.

Such was my thought before the testing time.

I tried my speed of foot against the princes,
And beat them both; we swam the river-whirlpool,
I beat them both; we wrestled, and I threw them.
Lastly, the Princess' Father bade them bring
The bow of the old hero of his House,
To try, if we could string it; they both failed.
I strung it, bent it, sent the screaming arrow
Into the blowing banner of my mark
So that I won the Princess, Rose of Women.

And then, before my triumph, there came this:
A sick man, mad with sorrow, was brought by
Beside his poor wife's corpse, a young thing, merry,
So the poor madman said, untimely dead.
And after them the madman's father came.
I saw the three:—Sickness, Old Age and Death,
The woe of Life, till then kept hidden from me.
I learned, for the first time, that I, Siddartha,

Being a Man, was chained unto the three.
That if I 'scaped the two, the third would have me.

When I had looked on Sickness, Age and Death
I could not live as Prince in happiness
While Man, my brother, suffered from such ill.
I thought, 'There must be healing for such pain.
If I go seek, I may discover it
And bring it to mankind.' So forth I went
With fellow-searchers, striving to find Peace.
I starved the rebel flesh till it shrank from me
Leaving me almost bone, while my mind strengthened.
I forced my mind to wring its evil from it.
Terrible agonies of body and mind
I beat myself to bear, but found no Peace,
Came to no Joy to gladden sorrowing man.
I could send forth my spirit like a bird
Over the waste, and in the waste it flew
But found no green leaf of delightful Peace.
With a clear mind I saw my withered flesh
As blackened skin upon a skeleton,
And knew that I had starved myself to death
For no bright gift of Joy, only despair.

Then I remembered that bright day of flowers
Near the calm water when my Joy had come.
And thought, "That day was Joy; today is Death.
Enlightenment can only come through Joy
I have gone into deserts to find Death."

Let all men praise the Woman who brings help.
There, as I lay a-dying in despair,

The bright Sujata and her Reaper passed.
Mercy and Light were in that woman's mind.
She saw what my companions would not see,
That I was dying in my misery.
She and her Reaper helped me to the shade,
She gave me milk and rice; she spoke such words
As came like rain upon my desert mind,
So that I cried, 'Leave me beneath this tree,
For I believe the Light will come to me.'

Under the tree my mind wrestled with death.
Light filled me with its agony of peace.

I saw Man in illusions of desire.
I knew my own illusions at an end
No stain of an illusion smirched my mind
It saw, it knew, it could; all powers it had.
In darkness and in brightness I saw lives,
My life, my former lives, my myriad lives,
Stretch back into the world's forgotten times,
To selfs long dead, when I was beast and bird,
Fish in the water, insects in the air,
Tree, shrub, or plant, or lichen on the stone,
Or unseen atom in a water-drop.
The iron of my evil fettering me,
The gold of my achievement freeing me.

Desire, longing for life, and ignorance,
Dropped from my mind like rags; I was set free,
I knew that I need never live again,
Save as a mind that with undying Peace
Moves among mortals in their misery
Shewing a way from darkness into light."

SHOPPING IN OXFORD

SHOPPING IN OXFORD

TWENTY-FOUR years ago, I wandered down
   An unknown, unseen, midnight Oxford Town,
And crossed the Thames, and paused upon the bridge
To note the smudge of wood on Hinksey Ridge;
Then went, by summer hedgerows, up the hill
In dewy dimness, all things lying still,
To hear the night-jars in the pine-wood spinning
And the first blackbird tell the day beginning.

Since then, my happy days have all been spent
By this gray town for Learning excellent;
Some of her scholars whom the world commends
Have been for years my neighbours and my friends.
As to the World and Time, she is to me
A Sovran City of Civility.

Others have told her power, who have known.
A vagrant, I, not rightfully her own,
Who draw from her not Learning, having none,
But yet the kindness shared with everyone,
The grace and beauty scattered up and down,
And this in special, single to the town,
That those within her shops in courtesy
Repay the buyers whatsoe'er they buy.

Twenty-four years of purchase, in amount,
Mean, many parcels more than I can count.

In all that little life-time, year by year,
The weekly wants have brought me shopping here.
And knowing buying thus, I wonder well
What sort of life it is, to stand and sell.

The sellers stand, to cherish all day long
The hundred wants of the demanding throng;
To bear, however much they inly burn,
The rude, the pert, the thruster out of turn;
The meddlesome, whose fidget-fingers change
The place of goods that daintinesses range;
The troublesome-fastidious whose desires
Are, to see all, yet never to be buyers;
Or, possibly still worse, the unprecise,
His want unclear, who makes the labour thrice.
And many others bring a special hell
Doubtless, sometimes, to those who stand to sell,
Who, whether well or ill, or hot or freezing,
Seek out the buyer's pleasure and are pleasing.

That they are pleasing, all who ever buy
In Oxford shops can surely testify:
Of all the shops I name or do not name
I and their other buyers can make claim
That, of our purchased parcels laid in pile,
Each one was rendered friendly, with a smile,
A charming word or jest that gave a grace
Of silver to the penny's commonplace,
So that a spirit companied the thing
Borne in the paper package tied with string,
So that it seemed a thing not bought and sold
But given, out of friendship and worth gold.

It is a pleasant pastime to go eyeing
Where things attract and tempt you into buying;
The dustless shining things which subtly wait
Yourself, the willing fish for this the bait.
Among these verses I have written down
The fruits of shopping about Oxford town,
Each with the happy memory of faces
Who greet me friendly at the customed places,
And of the streets in which the windows shine,
That are the magnets to these friends of mine;
For here, new pleasures purchasers attend,
They find the looked-for treasure and a friend.

I seek few treasures, except books, the tools
Of those celestial souls the world calls fools.
Happy the morning giving time to stop
An hour at once in Basil Blackwell's shop,
There, in the Broad, within whose booky house
Half England's scholars nibble books or browse.
Where'er they wander blessed fortune theirs,
Books to the ceiling, other books upstairs.
Books, doubtless in the cellar, and behind
Romantic bays where iron ladders wind,
And in odd nooks sometimes in little shelves,
Lintot's and Tonson's calf-bound dainty twelves.

Many fair windows look on Oxford streets
Bright to the passing fly with booky sweets,
I know of seven others, but, alas,
Prudence and taxes make one guard' e pass'.

If books be suns, there is a moon's delight
About the things which help a man to write,
There is a joy arranging like the cook

The many things which help to make the book,
The paper bluish, blue-lined, toughish, glazed,
Which (when I wrote with pens) I ever praised;
The canvas note-books, taking to the eyes,
The paste-pots precious in a last revise;
The black and scarlet inks, the pens they feed
Of metal, quill or glass, or gold or reed;
The blotting-paper, pink or white, which sips
The damps of Helicon with thirsty lips;
The rubber-bands, or metal-weights, which guard
The written chapter on its base of card;
The envelopes, of twenty different shapes,
Each gummy-tongued above a mouth that gapes,
Each with a void in which will some day lurk
The chaptered, numbered, named, completed work.
The crayons, too, blue, green and yellow-tipped,
Useful for marking bundled manuscript;
And things with ever brief but useful lives,
Pencils and little pocket paper-knives;
And, waiting still the Greek seal I affix,
Cardinal-coloured wax in slender sticks.

Then the black-bright, smooth-running, clicking, clean
Brushed, oiled and dainty typewriting machine,
With tins of ribbons waiting for the blows
Which soon will hammer them to verse and prose;
These and their plenishings, I love to tell them
And love the happy houses where they sell them.

Then, too, the Printers, piled up to the roofs
With old work done and drying poster proofs,
With letterings in red, announcements, sales,

And damp, smudged galleys fluttering from nails;
The perfume of the drug that poets drink
(The brew they sometimes die of), printers' ink;
And close at hand the music poets bless,
The lift and trample of the printing press.
What memories I have, correcting versions
Of proofs for Recitations and Diversions,
In days of peace when every year's July
Brought us a Festival of Poetry.

All who love books must love the Binder's skill
That fights all foes that work a volume ill,
That slays the boring worm and nulls the fox
(Who yellows leaves like lichen upon rocks);
That smooths the tattered, dog's-eared crumpled page,
That brightens youth and glorifies old age,
That keeps old leather sides upon their backs
And scorns to shear dear pages with his axe.
Maltbys, the binders, re-create books thus;
And many a royal binding glorious
Of blue morocco or white vellum pure
They have made fair, in beauty to endure.
And cases, too, they make, in which are slipped
Old printer's copy, type or manuscript,
There like the mummy of old joy, to wait
A maid's cremation in some unknown grate.
These things St Michael's binders subtly build
Of linened card, and having lettered, gild.
All these, it once has been delight to buy
As workman's fittings to the craft I ply.

Though books delight me, sometimes music seems
As sure a gateway to a world of dreams.
Therefore I sometimes tread romantic floors
Lined to the ceiling with recorded scores,
Where, each in's box, the music-lovers stay
Hearing ten tunes and wishing nine away.
There, as the artist must, I follow fast,
The one, though interrupted, to the last,
And bear its black disc home and set it going
And tread its peace in moonlights out of knowing.
That room of records keeps the faery keys
Of gardens lovelier than th' Hesperides,
Of wells more liquid with eternal thought
Than Lully drank of or de Leon sought;
Therefore I see no records lifted down
Without the thought: "There Joy goes into town".

And other tools I sometimes come to find;
Carpenter's tools delighting hand and mind;
Vices to clutch the work, and crows with claws,
And saws and tenon-saws and metal-saws;
Chisels and firmer chisels, gouges, clippers,
The tiniest brads, the neatest little nippers,
Minutest screw-eyes, nails and screws of brass,
And drills so subtle that they bend, alas.
And other goods I sometimes come to seek
Sticks of hard woods and little scraps of teak,
And thread of many sorts to be the rope
Aboard a model not yet more than hope;
The paints and brushes for her, and the oil
Which gives such polish after so much toil.

What fun to buy these things, and to have known
In him who sells skill greater than your own.

While life is energy and blood is red
Some parts of shopping must be daily bread:—
Therefore, I praise the bakehouse standing sentry
Close upon Gloucester Green at Friar's Entry,
Wherein one buys the crusty, fragrant, sweet,
Hot brown bread, "precious as the gods do eat".
And scones so full of symmetry and light
That the glad tooth is half afraid to bite;
And buns that make the questioning spirit see
All Chelsea ever was or Bath could be.

In praising bakers, let me also praise
Those who refresh the weary on their ways;
The Shamrock tea-rooms, up the narrow stairs,
What scones, what jellies and what jams are theirs.
There, as the weary rest in Gothic nooks,
They hear the Oxford bells and bless the cooks.

Man needs instruction, daily bread and rest;
Convention adds, he should be shod and dressed.
And England has a lack which all deplore,
The suit for work within and out of door;
Such as the French blue blouse or English smock
One not in use, the other not in stock.
Till lately, too, she kept a crazy rule,
"In summer seasons no man must be cool".
I was the first that order to defy,
I wandered cool in Oxford only I.

I praise the tailors who (perhaps in fear),
Helped this insane, wise, easy pioneer.
I well remember in that early stage
Men's angry envy or their jealous rage;
But I was cool and smiled to see the scowl
Glare from the furry coat and woollen cowl.
I bless the skilful men who keep my form
In summer tranquil and in winter warm.

Then those who during many years have shod
The feet upon whose leather I have trod,
In all five continents and seven seas
And twenty-six of man's communities.
Upon their leather, wheresoe'er I roam,
I have set forth and later wandered home
And ever find, re-entering the place
The same swift helpful tact and courteous grace.

Then those, across the way, that fragrant cave
Of joys of life and guards against the grave;
Whence, besides drugs, the buyer carries home
The sponge that sluices and the soaps that foam,
Throat-blessing gargles, and the scented, nice,
Pungent, sub-Tropic, cuttled dentifrice;
The shaving-brush whereon the lathers swoon
Being plucked at dawn from badgers of the Moon;
Boracic crystals, lint and cataplasms
And cures for all from pernio to spasms.

In Market Street, a glittering shop there is
Pounce-like and sharp with many cutleries
Of knives, and the most cunning scissors made,

And many a different kind of razor-blade.
Since edges have meant progress, sages stop
Always, to eye the wonders in this shop.

In many a morning I have gone to choose
Groceries, fruits and sweets at Grimbly Hughes,
That crowded house where all that man has dreamt
Of dainty niceness is in sight to tempt.
Then, the Cadena, crowded with the wise
Who seek fresh-ground the coffee that they prize
And bear it home in paper-bags imprest
Scenting the street with Araby the Blest.
There, too, a counter stands of sweet things sweeter
Than tongue can ever tell in words and metre.

Then in the Market there will always be
The stalls to tempt one, beautiful to see,
And to remember long in after hours
For some undreamed-of ecstasy of flowers,
Or some strange fruit, or subtle alien plant
Remote among her spines, perverse, askant;
Or rapturous words from little girls and boys
In Paradise from looking at the toys.
Even in time of war, the shops display
The wealth of sea and land in their array,
The sides of beef still dangle from the hooks;
The meat-axe chops for critic-witted cooks;
And damp on marble slabs the ice amid
The fish forget the pure through which they glid.

And other shops there are where none can pry
Unless with peril of a bankruptcy;
The charming shops of old and lovely gear

From what were homes of folk no longer here,
The chairs, the stuffs, the gems, the yellowed lace,
The fans once cool on some forgotten face;
The shawl where silken butterflies still glance
Whose owner saw Carlotta Grisi dance;
The dainty havings sadly left behind
By ancient love and elegance of mind;
The necklet-lockets still containing hair
From loves, now ghosts, long mingled in the air;
Enamelled boxes haunted by the faint
Sweet scent or tint of powder or of paint;
The netted purse, whose owner long since went
Under the spade, her last spade-guinea spent;
The miniatures, un-named, of folk unknown;
And saddest yet, the painted eye alone.
Among the gilt, the silk and old brocade
Of ruined homes which past affections made,
Sometimes a mirror, chair, or broidered piece,
Is singled thence, to take another lease
Of human use and sometimes seekers' eyes
Searching the print-pile come upon a prize
A Dürer or a Rembrandt; or a drawing
Of ships disdainful of the billows clawing
(Such prizes have been mine) , and sometimes, too,
Among the porcelain, all white and blue,
Of early Worcester, one perceives the bowl,
The bell-like, swan-like, chipless, crackless, whole
Desired piece that summer's fragrant stir
Shall fill with rose-leaves or with lavender.

The common thing, if blessed by head and heart,
Becomes uncommon as a work of art;

So these who sell to those who only buy
Have made their sellings bright in memory.
Thanks cannot pay what kindness freely gives,
But the glad kindness runs the world and lives.
I live the gladder for the daily thought
"They gave me golden what my copper bought."

MAHDAMA'S QUEST

MAHDAMA'S QUEST

THE moon had kept the world awake,
   The herons filled the marsh with cry,
Prince Mahdama lay sick with ache
For love of Princess Malati.

He saw the moon burn into ember
And other lights in Heaven shone.
His spirit struggled to remember
The image of her beauty gone.

Until, as the False Morning whitened,
A wind about the palace eaves
Blew cool, and all the fruit-trees brightened,
Turning the silver sides of leaves.

Then, whether he were wake or dreaming,
He could not tell, he could but stare
For surely, by the fountain gleaming,
The Princess Malati was there.

He thrust aside the clicking curtain,
He strode into the dusk to see.
He said "Who are you?" He was certain,
Or was he certain? it was she.

He took a step towards her, saying
"Princess, Princess, what is it, speak."

Her hands were stretched, as if in praying.
And tears were gleaming on her cheek.

It was herself, though white and broken,
Her very self; but, as he neared,
The words "For pity . . . save" . . . were spoken
And then she dimmed and disappeared.

Dimmed through the water-droplets falling
In silver from their lapsing tree . . .
He cried "Is it your spirit calling . . .
In deadly peril, calling me?

Ah, this is vision and deceiving
But I must ride at once"; he rode
With heart despairing and sighs heaving
For Princess Malati's abode.

Towards him, spurring through the morning
He met her servant, hurrying on.
Crying "I ride to bring you warning . . .
The Princess Malati is gone.

Before the daybreak, word was brought her
Her foster-mother, stricken dumb,
Besought by signs her darling daughter
For Heaven's pity's sake to come.

She went alone; within the hour
We learned the message false; and since
Our searching-parties ride to scour
The ways for her; come, help us, Prince."

They rode the dairy-meadows, questing.
They searched the outland farms in vain.
Some tried the easting, some, the westing,
Mahdama called "I'll try the plain".

"The plain", they answered. "None would ride there.
The Princess least of all; beside . .
The Powers of the Dark abide there . .
There is no track, and none will guide."

He said "It is the one remaining
Way to her friend, not yet explored".
He rode alone back to the laning
That led through jungle to the ford.

Up, from the brake, the wild-duck scuttered,
Up, in a V, into the sky.
The river wimpled, the reeds fluttered,
The reed-birds breathed their warning cry.

There lay the little-ridden hithing;
Beyond, the reed-beds stood up still
With some leaves trembling, some leaves writhing
At the water's impulse and wind's will.

He eyed the brake beyond the water;
The reed-birds flitted without fears;
No ambush waited there to slaughter,
And yet his horse pricked up his ears.

Nay, sniffed, and stiffened as he eyed it,
That wall of wavering green-gray,

[27]

Something uncanny was inside it,
That sent a warning on the way.

So, tense, he crossed the ford, not doubting
That something evil lay beyond.
The long-tailed harebell-birds were scouting
For water-flies among the frond.

The long-tailed little blue-birds scattered;
The narrow trackway opened wide,
There, dead among the reed-stalks shattered,
The Princess' mare lay on her side.

She had been shot and then forsaken,
The lovely Moonlight, the white mare.
Doubtless, the Princess had been taken,
Many men's feet had trampled there.

There they had crouched in covert, hiding,
The tale was written for his eyes.
Thither the Princess had come riding,
Thence they had galloped with their prize.

He cantered on after the reivers
To all things but their traces blind.
Inly he withered with the fevers
That gnaw within a lover's mind.

The country which he rode grew stranger,
The strange died into the unknown.
But what are wounds and death and danger
When love is burning in the bone?

When western skies grew gold and greener
And stretching tigers 'gan to stir,
And first the burning air grew keener
He came upon a trace of her.

A scrap of blue and golden weaving
Had caught upon a jungle thorn.
Past any question of deceiving
It was a stuff which she had worn.

It was a silk; herself had decked it
With broidered birds; and cruel force,
Ruthless, alone could thus have wrecked it
Galloping by upon a horse.

The woods thinned out, the traces thickened,
More men had joined the robber band.
Here they had shaken out and quickened
To gallop into open land.

And, as the sun set, lo, a fastness,
Of tumbled stone, long since decayed;
Beyond, a downland in its vastness
Towards an endless Heaven strayed.

No love nor any raider shewed there,
The tracks led on into the down.
What were the standing stones that glowed there
Like doorways in a burning town?

Surely, those giant stones resembled
A place described in many a tale

At which the flesh of hearers trembled
And pulses leapt and cheeks were pale.

Surely within them lay an altar
Rough-hewn for many a bloody rite
Where dying moanings made the psalter
To praise its lord, the god of Night.

The tracks seemed to lead past the highland
Whereon those stones of horror stood;
The downland swelled there to an island;
The sunset glowered red as blood.

He thought: "I cannot follow further
These tracks, by sight, I'll turn aside
Enter that temple of old murther,
And pray the god to be my guide.

For it is said, that those imploring
In agony of prayer, may hear
With sound of moan and clash of warring,
The very god of Night draw near,

Who, if man's blood and hair are proffered
Three hours before the cock can crow,
Will touch and take the tribute offered
And tell him what he seeks to know.

I will implore the god; tomorrow,
If the god speaks, I shall be sure
What certainty I have of sorrow,
What possibility of cure."

A darkness breathed upon the burning;
He made the temple stones his mark.
His horse and he went trembling, learning
The many murders of the dark.

The stalkers of the night were creeping,
Death hovered on a noiseless wing,
The cries came of the victims' weeping.
He halted at the temple ring.

He picketed his horse and harkened.
No sound of human being stirred.
He fancied that the darkness darkened
And something breathed a whispered word.

Like gallowses, in part dismembered
The granites of the temple ran;
As places will, that place remembered
The evil stamped on it by man.

What was it? Was the night-wind making
Cry, or were watchers drawing breath?
He knew not which, but entered, quaking
The circle of that church of death.

Within, with whimpering and moaning,
The night-wind seemed to search the night,
Now, like a temple-priest intoning,
Now, like a cut-throat stepping light.

Guessing his way, he groped and fumbled
Across that darkness filled with moan

Till at the circle's heart he stumbled
Upon the earth-laid altar-stone.

That was the spot, whereon, for ages,
Men had implored their darkest thought
And paid down human blood as wages
To lure the horror that they sought.

"Here I must ask for help" he muttered.
"Here I must offer blood and hair,
And pray". . . . He left the rest unuttered
For things with lights were coming there.

What was it, that was coming nearer?
Some wandering lights there seemed to glide,
Then hesitate, then glitter clearer,
Then sway a little to the side.

What were those lights, advancing, pausing?
Blood-seeking moths, or bats, or birds?
What silent murder were they causing?
What thought ran in them without words?

Surely, those sideway darts and leapings
Were springs from things with tooth and claw
Snatching to drink the hot blood's seepings
At urge of some inhuman law.

They paused, then on, and now a drumming
Mixed with a clacking as of bone,
Told him that these were mortals coming
To feast the midnight altar-stone.

And now, with pans of fire rushing
Strange shapes in red sped to the ring,
The sparks out of the pans went gushing
Like wasps of fire on the wing.

Dog-headed were these shapes, and yapping
Like bandogs starved of blood; they stood
Within the ring of sarsens, snapping,
Lit by their fires, red as blood.

Mahdama crouched beside the table
At which the night god ate and drank.
The dog-heads yapped and sparked; the babel
Of drum and clacking rose and sank.

Now, with wide-swinging lanterns, slowly,
The dancers entered to their rite;
Creatures in black and red, unholy,
Were dragging forward one in white.

The clack kept time; their lights and censers
Shot sideways, back, then glittered on;
They danced in little steps, like fencers;
Pale fire round their leader shone.

Till, lo, the evil altar nearing,
They halted, and a hymn began,
The utterance of all the fearing
In all the midnight of a man.

As Mahdama crouched, watched and listened
A striped thing headed like a beast

[33]

Laid on the altar knives which glistened
And lights came forward for the priest.

The priest drew to the altar, lifting
A call which struck the singers dumb;
A flying moon broke through the rifting,
The time of sacrifice had come.

Man-tigers dragged the white form nearer
As victim on that stone to lie.
Mahdama saw the figure clearer
It was his darling, Malati.

Then dancers hurtled round the altar,
Mewing, and beating discs that clanged.
Mahdama's spirit did not falter,
He took the death-knife, toothed and fanged.

He leaped upon the altar, crying
"I am the Power whom you call.
I am the dealer of Man's dying;
Death, the destroyer of you all."

They moaned with terror as they harkened.
He cried, "You flying Moon, make dark".
Cloud quenched the moon, the temple darkened.
He leapt and struck the high-priest stark.

And lifting Malati, he bade her,
"Have no more terror now; come on".
Then swiftly, with his arm to aid her,
Out of the temple they were gone.

He set her on the horse, and taking
A rein in hand, he ran beside.
Out of the cloud the moon came breaking,
The plain before them opened wide.

The moon came flying out to wreath them,
A cock crew for the coming day,
Out of the downland grass beneath them
Bewildered beetles sped away.

Before the Sun, then swiftly springing,
Had sunken to his rest in red,
The City bells were set a-ringing,
The Princess and the Prince were wed.

AN ART WORKER

AN ART WORKER

WHEN St John's chimes for Ten
I greet that chief of men
Sir Mahlstick Tubes, R.A.,
To whom I sit all day,
As Christian Martyr scorned,
As Beauty Unadorned,
As Niobe who mourned,
As any famous She
Whom Tubes wants me to be
From any sort of time
In any kind of clime,
Under the snow or sun
In costume or in none.

I will say this for Tubes,
He doesn't paint me in cubes,
Nor as a cupboard broken,
With half its drawers pulled open,
Nor as a question mark
Mixed up with bits of shark,
Some music and a shoe,
As lots of them might do.
He thinks me, I believe,
A fair daughter of Eve
Whom his great mind will hallow
Into a thing of tallow.

[39]

At five, I hear him say
"That will do for today.
Tomorrow morning, at Ten".

I dress and leave him then.

He goes to tea and rest.
When he has bathed and dressed,
His Wife is newly gowned,
His shiny car comes round.
Himself glossy and shiny,
In expectation of dine-y
With cocktail of sherry wine-y.
Away they drive in the dark
To some big house near the Park,
Where I, as Tamar or Leah,
Or Helen, or Amalthea,
Or wonder of other nation,
Am part of the decoration.
There let him talk till one
Of Art achieved and undone.

I, who have left him thus,
Hurry aboard a bus,
Up to the roof, and there
Watch, for a copper fare,
Sunset, west of the chimneys
Putting red in the dimness,
Sometimes herons in flight
Bound for a reed-grown eyt,
To stand knee-deep through the night
In Colne, Kennet or Thame
Whom change leaves ever the same.

Sometimes the windows burn,
Or wind-vanes gleam as they turn,
Or little boys in a race
Rush, with light in the face.
They are such happy ones
I wish that they were my sons.

Then, what a joy, as light
Makes the shop-windows bright,
Shops like welcome to Kings
With all bright beautiful things,
Which Kings would covet to buy
Were they as happy as I,
Only to give, to give,
To make some gladder to live.

Now the bus halts; again
I climb the dark little lane,
Take the blind little turning :—
There is the window burning.
A step runs to my knock,
A hand turns at the lock.
I enter; the latch clicks,
St Mary's chimes for Six.
My lover and I are one;
Now the day has begun.

First, he will show and say
What he has done today
Upon the work in hand.

The task that he has planned
Is, to paint twenty scenes
Of what today's life means

To us, the young, who tread
As heirs to all Earth's dead,
Through London Town today.

What twenty would you choose,
You, in my lover's shoes?

These scenes are in his plan:—
Ten toils of labouring Man;
Essential Labour such
As no time alters much.
Ten scenes from tale and myth,
That Man still comrades with;
Such as should deck the wall
In School or City Hall,
'Change, Library or Bank,
Now, usually, left blank.

First, the ten toils beginning
With Bread through all its winning,
From plough-man in the acre
To reaper, miller and baker,
The last with head bent down
Watching his batch turn brown.

Next, shearers, cobblers and weavers,
Stone-cutters and wood-cleavers,
Builders of homes of men
Work done agen and agen,
To house, clothe, shoe and feed
Adam's swift leaf-brief seed.

Next, the ten tales that still
Have living power to thrill :—
The Man born to be King :—
The Statue wed with the Ring :—
The square of Priam's Court
With Hektor's last fight fought,

With Hektor dead i' the wain
Brought home to Troy again;
The King and the dumb crowd;
Three Queens crying aloud,
One, for a child left lone,
One, from a heart made stone,
One, from self-pity and shame.

Cassandra shrinks from the flame.

Then four old tales of ours,
English as Berkshire flowers,
The tale that Shropshire told
Of pure Sabrina of old,
Pursued by bloodhounds grim
To raddled Severn's brim,
Calling the god to save,
Then plucked to his green cave
To be with him forever,
Queen of the Shropshire River,
With her bright damozils
The brooks out of the hills.

Arthur's and Modred's bands
In fight on Camlan Sands,

The last men left of each.
The Queens' barge off the beach;
And, in the rocks, the Past,
Claiming her sword at last.

The Fruit, Eternal Life,
Which Marc gave to his Wife,
And she, to Tristan the brave,
And he to Brangwen gave,
And she, back to King Marc,
Who went out into the dark
And gave it to a poor
Sick woman at his door.

Then Francis Drake, long since,
There, with the Maroon Prince
High in the skysaild tree
Watching the Southern Sea,
And seeing there unfold
The English quest for gold,
The reachings and the rakings
Of all our galleon takings,
And more, his valour's heir
Founding new Nations there,
New Nations, such as men
Had never dreamed of then.

His seamen lure with bread
The parrots blue and red
And offer English pennies
To the brown piccaninnies.
The piebald monkies loot
The Maroons' frails of fruit.

Gautama lying prone
A wreck of skin and bone,
His body broken and dulled,
His search for light annulled.
The monks, his friends, as one
Thinking his struggle done.
Then she, with milk in pail,
With rice and cakes in frail,
Stooping to give him strength
That he beholds at length
The Enemies, yet sees
Things brighter, conquering these.
And shapes of light drawn near
To bless and crown the Seer.

The broad-leaved tree gives flower
Knowing the holy hour.

Then Ross, that man of Hope,
Bent at his microscope
After so many a check
Seeing the changing speck
That laid the secret bare
Of Death riding the air
Blasting the garden of earth,
O glad day of new birth.

Lastly, an end of Night,
The gray rocks taking light;
Upon the olive treen
A dewy silver-green;
The things of darkness shrink.

By the tomb-door, a link
Burned-out, droops in its ring.
A cock there shakes his wing.

The April flowers are sparse,
A blackthorn, with white stars,
Some daffodils, and studs
Of green, where a thorn buds.

Distant, behind, below,
The City ramparts glow;
The light shines on the rock
Behind the crowing cock.
The carvings of gods gone
Egypt and Babylon.

In blankets, sleeping hard,
The sergeant and his guard.
One waken sentry shy
Startles, to find drawn nigh
Mary, and friends with her
With frankincense and myrrh,

So, then, I first look over
The day's work of my lover;
Pondering, I suggest
What might make better best.
We plan the show to be
When all the world will see
These twenty on the wall
And hurry to buy all.
Sometimes we find a cheer
Supposing the time here
When every building glows

To give joy as Man goes
With stories in the sun
Companioning each one.

Someday, beyond all doubt,
When folly's day is out
And wisdom's day is in
Such methods will begin
In London and elsewhere
With great tales painted fair
Wherever a great mass
Of folk will meet and pass.
For someday, the blank wall
Distempered white, will pall.
Someday the cry will be
For something fair to see.
Someday a Corporation
Will up and save the Nation
By giving vivid life
To citizen and wife . . .
Meanwhile, on the small scale
My lover tells his tale.

Next, to our evening meal
At Jules', the Spinning Wheel,
In Playmate Street, Soho,
Where all our party go.
Our friends will all be there
In cigarette-thick air.
The plates clack, the folk feed,
The waiters move with speed,
Crying their kind of tune :—

"Un Château La Lagune.
Biftek un . . Encore une . .
Un côté . . un gigot . .
Un Punch . . Des escargots . . ."

Painters, sculptors, engravers,
All of the salt with savours,
Writers of verse and prose,
Men whom nobody knows
Except ourselves, who are sure
That they will grow and endure.
    We, who are young, contain
    The new germ in the brain
    Whose influence will be
    The new time's ecstasy
    Of greater joy to live
    Radiant and positive
    Spite of the mumbling mass
    Of john ox and jack ass.
There's none, of the Jules' set,
Whose face you would forget,
Each soul is set to say
The new word the new way.
And what is the new word
But April to the bird?
A statement of delight
In life and love and light?
That Art in everyone
Is something of the Sun,
Delighting, cheering, living,
Exalting and forgiving,
Colouring, making glad,

Leaving the dead, the mad,
The sick, the sour, the sad,
First to the medicine maker,
Then, to the undertaker,
For all those five and Art
Are all the poles apart.

These thoughts are deep instilled
As base on which to build,
Art is the Sun which shines.

But here at Jules' one dines,
And many a merry quip
Goes between cup and lip.
What comment and what fun
About work lately done
What judgment and what wit
What portraits neatly hit,
What plans for the Review
That shall be something new
With that strange tale of C's
With those designs of D's;
And three of F's etched heads;
The tale in verse of Z's;
U's sonnets and Y's prose;
The treasure-box of O's.

These things we all debate
Betwixt the cup and plate

Then, having dined, we go
Through Soho to the show,
The music-hall or play,
Now thrilling London clay.

Or the great concert-room
With organ-pipes in gloom
Where some Quartet is more
Like one man's play than four;
Or flame-haired pianist
With steel springs in his wrist
And fire in his fingers
Asserts the plea that lingers.

Sometimes, we climb long stairs.
The orchestra prepares,
The red sail-curtain droops
With dull gold done in loops;
And in the crack before us
Some shining shoes of chorus.
The eighty players tune :—
It will be Seville soon,
Seville in Andaluth,
In love, in passionate youth.

But the delight most dear
Comes seldom in the year
When shines the happy star
And Russian Ballets are.
No other art so fair
Is with us anywhere,
So when it comes we hie
Gladly tow'rds bankruptcy.

But when it rains and snows,
Or fogs, or a gale blows,
We build the studio fire
To whiter-heat and higher;

I cook the fragrant dish
Of buttered eggs or fish;
He makes the toast; I brew
A coffee given to few;
Then, having washed and cleared,
The filthy night is cheered.

    We draw beside the blaze,
    He takes some book of plays,
    Or Chaucer, Milton or Keats.
    He reads, while the storm beats,
While the hob-kettle mizzles
The roasting chestnut sizzles,
The mind within his voice
Makes every rhythm rejoice.

    Or each a pasture finds
    In new books by new minds
    Or old books of a lure
    Forever sweet and sure
    Cervantes, Burton, Gray . .
    (Dickens for holiday).

Or, if the books not cheer,
We have our comfort here.
We fix our model stage
On which our dolls engage
In setts of painted ply;
Designers, he and I;
We re-tell and re-dress
Romantic loveliness;
All the best fables known
We have re-made and shewn.

Our blithest joy is this;
Our very dream it is
To see our story thus
Made live and glorious
Upon some English stage,
A book's bright painted page
Alive with sweeping swarms
Of exquisite lithe forms.
Well, what the artists see
Must someday come to be.
Meantime, we pose and plan
The best scenes known to man.

Sometimes our friends are here
For good talk wild and dear,
Of art done or to be,
Of work to read or see;
And one brings his design,
To shew this man of mine.
We judge it line by line.
One reads a tale or play.
One has some verse to say,
And one with strings or flute
Leaves us so thrilled and mute
We only inly ask
Such mood for our life's task.
One sometimes brings to show
His rare portfolio
Etchings or drawings all
Found at some sale or stall
Or in some dingy box
Of books all gone to fox,

Or marine-store decayed
With whom the burglars trade.
It is a pleasure rare
To see these and compare
Our own rare bargains found
In London's hunting-ground;
The Melencolia print;
The Lucas mezzotint;
The seven Liber plates;
The Meryon early states;
The Sheffield tea-pot white;
And my most dear delight
The Etty portrait ta'en
In Smithfield, in the rain,
Beneath a naphtha flare
Upon a barrow there,
Midst cracked red bedroom glass,
And bits of harness-brass
And books with covers loose
And pewter out of use,
And old brass candlesticks.
Its price was three and six,
But I paid only three
"Because it is like me"
A lady of desire
Gazing upon a fire,
Black dress and red divan,
A joy to any man.
And I, I found her, I
With my quick little eye.

When the first swallow shy
First haunts the dusk, we hie
To see the maiden veil
Of plum-bloom lying pale
Upon the trees' green polls
What time the cuckoo tolls.

And when the scarcely borne
White fleece is on the thorn
May's maiden raiment
Rich-incense-thick in scent,
We go upstream and boat
Watching our image float
Where written ripples drag
At roots of yellow flag,
And water-rats swim by
Quaking the mirrored sky,
And the harsh heron flogs
Blue pinions as he shogs.
Or, while the thorn's a priest
We go where bricks have ceased
To woods where moonlight dapples
The bluebells with her apples
And dim deer step the blanch
Never snapping the branch.

These jaunts of dear delight,
On Sundays and at night
Are done with extreme thrift.
I plan and scheme and shift;
Each penny goes with plan
Of how to serve my man,

To give him beauty and peace
While his great gifts increase,
While his intense eye keen
Takes something from things seen,
To make more poignant still
An image of his will.

Sometimes, instead, we seek
The crowd-life at its peak.
The salesmen shouting wares
Under the naphtha flares
In markets jammed with stalls
Where gong clangs and man bawls
And women finger and cheapen
That fourpen' may be threepen'
Oranges, rabbits, meat,
Dates, pulped to sticky sweet,
Violets, cabbage, toys,
All colour, movement, noise.

Sometimes we seek the anger,
The shatter of bells and clangour
Of fire-engines at speed
Hurtling to help man's need.
The sparks flash at the curve,
The lines of helmets swerve,
The crowd runs, the smoke pours
Flame fills windows and doors.
Or on some football field
We watch the thousands steeled,
Watching one, prone on's face
Ready to set the place,

[55]

While in the autumn sun
The kicker nerves for's run.

There, in the goal, in line,
The fifteen wait the sign . . .
And see . . the ball goes down . . .
A great gasp takes the town,
Kicker and foemen rush.
The ball goes up in a hush . .
Up, in a quake of soul as . .
It hits the post, and . . Goal.

Or in the Spring, we go
To Kew, as the bulbs blow
To see what lovely thing
Shall deck the Queen of Spring
And what small flowers sweet
Shall be about her feet
In that fair Dream of May
His genius will portray.
The great flowers and tiny
The stalks erect or twiney
The soft-leaved and the spiny.
All are new facets bright
Of everlasting light.
So at the Zoo the strange
Fish, birds and beasts who range,
With swift fin, wing and paw,
Are light prisoned in law,
Each with a beauty dear,
My lover shall make clear.

What gay life looks at us
From the convolvulus
And what red force of Mars
From the tiger's prison-bars.

    But most we love returning
    To the small fire burning,
    Through the deserted town
    The lamp-light dwindled down,
    Through starlit street and square
    In the night's smokeless air,
    Hardly a window glowing
    None, but the night-cat, going
    (Save, afar-off, the feet
    Of pointsman on his beat),
    Each of us thinking Bed,
    The eyelids touched with lead,
    The intellect released
    By sleep, healer and priest,
    To Dream where splendours make
    Wonders for when we wake.

A mouse runs in the walls,
A coal in the grate falls,
Without, no noise of men.
One distant voice, Big Ben,
Calling, then falling still,
    Quiet are want and will,
    Away, the self and greed
    Of every artist's need;
    All is resolved and laid

New lavendered, remade,
Sure to be brighter,
When it is lighter.

When morning brings the day
I am a drapered clay
To Mahlstick Tubes, R.A.,
Who makes me War or Peace
In his mind's candle-grease.